Real Poems for Real Moms

REAL POEMS FOR REAL MOMS

from a mother in the trenches to another

RACHEL S. DONAHUE

Jessie —
Thank you for being an encouragement in the trenches. Press on, friend! Be encouraged!

Donahue Daily Creative
www.thedonahuedaily.com

Real Poems for Real Moms: from a Mother in the Trenches to Another
Copyright © 2019 Rachel S. Donahue. All rights reserved.

"First Day in Ramah" Copyright © 2019 Daniel A. Speer, used with permission.

All rights reserved. This book or any portion thereof may not be reproduced, photocopied, pictographed, etched in stone, fire-branded, tattooed, landscaped, painted on a grecian urn, or used in any manner whatsoever (except for the use of brief quotations in a book review or free advertisement through social media posts tagging the author) without the express written permission of the publisher. Penalties for violations shall include but not be limited to babysitting the author's children without payment.

Title design and cover hand-drawn by Katie Brunone Illustration
Dahlia illustration and back page design by Sofia Rector, @artadorningthedark
Other interior illustrations by Rachel S. Donahue

Flourishes designed by freepik.com
Type set in Fontin and Fontin Sans

Printed in the United States of America

First Printing, 2019

ISBN 978-0-578-44198-6

Donahue Daily Creative
P.O. Box 2473
Indian Trail, NC 28079

www.thedonahuedaily.com

3 . 14 15 9 26 53 58 9 7 9 32 38 46 26 43 3 8 32 79 50 28 84 19

For my mother,
who first introduced me to words
and encouraged my love of them,

And for Lanier Ivester,
whose thoughtful words
first prompted me
to pen a few of my own.

With thanks to all the Rabbits:
you give me courage.

8 December, 2018
Indian Trail, North Carolina

Dear Reader,

Not long ago I woke up to the realization of two things: one, that I had been changing diapers for more than ten years straight; and two, that I had somehow lost myself to the daily demands of motherhood. Our family had just experienced an upheaval of all we had known to that point, and for the first time in our marriage my husband and I were no longer working together side by side—he was gone to work long hours every day while I was left alone with the children with no purpose outside the four walls of our home. I felt like every single ounce of my existence was being wrung out like a pile of clothes in the laundry sink.

Do you know the feeling? It's a lot like waking up to a toddler standing three inches from your face: a moment of panic, deep breaths to calm the heart rate, and a quandry of what to do next.

I desperately asked God to help me be content in my roles as wife and mother, to keep me faithful in this hard season. To some degree, He answered that prayer, graciously giving me the daily manna I needed to press on—but I still suffered from a nagging restlessness. Looking back, I'd call it a holy restlessness.

I was tempted to flee my responsibilities in an empty pursuit of diversions and call it "me time," but I knew the end of that path, and it's not contentment. So instead I allowed my restlessness to drive me to seek the heart of my Father without distraction (read: a week-long electronics fast) to ask for His direction for me and my brood of children in this lonely season. And there, in the quiet, He did a surprising thing: He brought me back to the passions that spurred my studies and delighted my soul long before I had kids.

Soon I began to devour poetry and classic novels and stories of all kinds for the first time since college—just for the sheer joy of it. Every time I sat down to nurse the baby, I put down my phone and picked up a book. My mind was engaged in new ways, and my entire being felt nourished, even as I continued to pour myself out for my family. The Bible began to come alive for me in new ways, too, as my imagination was stirred by the variety of things I was reading. My soul filled to the brim and began to spill over—into poetry of my own. In two days' time I had half a dozen poems and a fun new hobby. What did I write about, you may ask? Motherhood, mostly. It's what I know best.

This whole process has been life-giving. My circumstances haven't changed much, but I do find something to appreciate in them (most of the time). Even bad days can make for a good poem. It's all about perspective.

After two years of poeming amidst the laundry and the dishes and the endless hours of rocking the baby, I've amassed a little collection. The poems still delight me, so I figured I should share this delight with someone else. I'm sure I'm not the only one who needs encouragement.

Motherhood is messy and demanding, but it is a high calling—a high calling, indeed. Hang in there, dear reader. You are not alone. These poems have been a gift to me, and now they are a gift to you—from one mother in the trenches to another.

Be encouraged,

Rachel S. Donahue

Table of Contents

Abundance	1
On Blueberries	3
The Blue Line	4
Dimpled Beauty	5
Diaper Haiku	6
When You Wake	7
Mom Guilt	8
Rough and Tumble	10
Salvation	12
Little Bird	13
Hunger	14
Diaper Haiku II	16
Mid-night Sonnetesque	17
Sweetie	18
Boy Sonnet	19
Kisser of Knees	20
A TCK Mom Dilemma	21
It's Going to Be a Good Day	22
Diaper Haiku III	23
Too Quiet?	24
In the Silence	25
Unlucky	26
Whosoever Planteth a Tree	27

Summer Storm	28
On the Paradox of Sleep	30
Diaper Haiku IV	31
It's Too Private	32
The Blue Car	33
Another Morning	35
Days of the Week	36
Sustenance	37
The Law of Inevitability	38
I Wonder	39
Shucking Corn	41
Hide and Seek	42
Fun	44
Diaper Haiku V	45
True Love	46
Failure	48
Wiping	51
Trampoline	53
At the Beach	54
What I Meant to Say	56
Disaster	57
Lost	58
Going Somewhere	59
Little One Lost	60
First Day in Ramah	61
Flower of Mine	62
What This Mother Needs	63
Back in the Day	64
Diaper Haiku VI	65

Smiles I	66
Off Day	67
Diaper Haiku VII	68
Found	69
Laundry Day	70
It's Only a Season	71
I Wanted to Write a Poem	72
Smiles II	73
How I Will Be Remembered	74
Transformation	75
On Waiting In Line	76
Suggested Reading	79

Abundance

A Spring
bubbles up
from beneath,
filling a pool
until its heavy brim
spills over
liberally
into another.

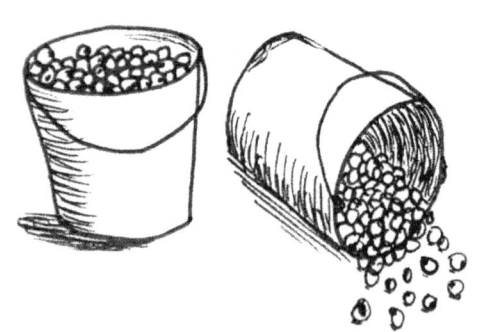

On Blueberries

My boys eat blueberries like candy.
I'd rather they eat blueberries than candy.

> We buy them in large bags, freshly frozen,
> And we pour them liberally,
> Summer's bounty in a midwinter bowl.

One child—
He who likes sameness and predictability—
Asks for them daily.
For health and possibility and love, I oblige.

> As I thaw another handful under the cool flow of water,
> I suddenly remember
> The prick of bushes,
> Sweetness wafting on the air,
> And a steep descent.

The heat, the sweat, the weight, the work—
All for a small pail of goodness
To be picked through and washed and savored.

> I am suddenly aware of our family's wealth
> And our poverty.

Even as I rejoice over the goodness I hold
And the relative ease of such provision,
I mourn that my children are so disconnected from its Source.

> I resolve to take them blueberry picking—
> Once ice thaws and green returns to earth—
> Just as my own mother once took me.

I understand now:
It wasn't just for the blueberries.

The Blue Line

so much depends
upon

a thin plastic
stick

lined with
blue

beside the bathroom
sink

Dimpled Beauty

Glory be to God for dimpled things—
  For hands too small proportioned, fleshy, round;
    For cheeky laughs outside parentheses of grins;
Tight cherubbed hugs, though lacking wings;
  Stout knees that meet too often with the ground;
    And raspberried bellies, once hidden, sought again.

All things budding, bright, ruddy, flush,
  Whatever pure, plump, petite dear thing be found,
    Both bonny and chubby, delight of kith and kin,
He fathers-forth to fathers, mothers—
  Hush—
    Praise Him.

Diaper Haiku

How many colors
can a newborn baby boy
produce in a day?

When You Wake

This is my favorite time-with-you of day,
These moments just after you wake
With the pink flush of sleep
Upon your cheeks
And the glisten of a tear
Caught in the round place
Beside your nose.
Your lashes bat away the light
That brightens blue your slumbered eyes
As you up-reach two dimpled hands
And sweetly call my name.
I pull your tiny frame up,
Up into my arms and you
Golden-nestle your softly tousled head
Upon my chest
And rest
Until the siren call of play
Gently beckons you away
And you scramble from my arms
To leave.

Mom Guilt

Mom guilt.
I can't shake it.
It's there every time I turn around.

What my kids eat.
What *I* eat.
What we *should* be eating but we don't.
Organic? GMOs? Antibiotics and growth hormones?
Stress.
Sometimes I just want Oreos.

Milestones and growth charts.
Do we vaccinate or not?
Babywearing. Sleep habits.
Breastfeeding. Bottle feeding.
Stress.
I should be savoring these moments, right?
Sometimes I just want to sleep.

Looks from other moms at the playground.
Judgment from older folks at a restaurant.
Advice from a lady with three dogs and no kids.
Stress.
Some days I just want to hide at home.
(But then I feel lonely.)

Laundry piles. I'm so behind.
To-do lists and *should*-do lists.
How to clean, what to clean, when to clean, and why.
Kitchen, bathrooms, bedrooms, living area, repeat.
There's never an end to bringing order.
Something always seems to suffer.
Some days that something is me.

Homework battles.
Homework battles!
When will summer be here?
When will summer be over?

They've been on screens too long.
Have they played outside?
How long have they been reading?
Academics. Sports. Therapies. Lessons.
Stress.
I just want to let my kids be kids.

Mom guilt.
I can't shake it.
It's there every time I turn around.
But so is grace.

Rough and Tumble

Rough and tumble—crash!—there goes
My coffee cup. I sigh and know
They won't clean up the mess they've made,
No, not without my guiding aid.

I put the laundry down and breathe—
I calm myself because I need
To temper what I'm wont to yell.
It's simmering there; I feel it swell.

I halt my steps a moment more
Not to react as oft before.
I pray for grace for me, for them.
(How oft I need this little gem!)

And then I head, quick, down the stairs
To find six little eyes, three chairs
And toys amuck across the floor
All spilling from the pantry door
Where hideouts burrow with the food.
The eyes are searching Momma's mood.

Drawing closer now, I spy
The candy wrappers which belie
The broken rule (or two, or three)
And who-done-it's no mystery.

I sigh once more with teeth clenched tight,
Containing rage with all my might.
With hands in fists I close my eyes—
To open them again, surprised
By hugs from one, then two, then three,
Mere boys who grin up sheepishly.

"I love you, Mom," they say sincerely.
Lord, to think that I so nearly
Tore them down with my harsh words,
A pecking good from Mother Bird.

I melt and hug them back, but still
Remind them of the rules until
I hear myself repeat His mandate:
"If you love me, keep my commandments."

Salvation

Lidded thermal mug,
Once again
Amidst the busyness of life
You save a sip of warmth
For that much-delayed moment
When I need it most.

Little Bird

Little cautious bird of brown and blue,
Stealing through my yard in search of treasure,
Dost thou know thy loving Father gives?
He nurtures thee with riches beyond measure!

Hunger

"I'm hungry, Mom."
The statement heaps a heavy bag of stress upon my back,
Weighing my steps to the kitchen—again.

"Is it time to eat yet?"
The question presses me hard
Into the cleft of stone and stone.

"What can I have to eat?"
The iteration latches on,
Bleeds my soul dry.

The leech has two daughters:
Give and Give.
I have three sons and a daughter:
Hungry, Hungry, Hungry, and Hungee.

I am empty,
Hollow,
Broken open,
Poured out,
Used up,
Wasted,
Spent.

My soul thirsts—
For You
                              I long to see your power and your glory

My flesh longs—
For You
                     In a dry and thirsty land where there is no water

           In this arid land of Motherhood,
             I know my children's hunger.

God,
My God,
I'm hungry.

Fill me,
Full up.
Overflow my cup.

And give me something good to feed my children.

Diaper Haiku II

Once carefree was I—
necessary excrement,
how you've changed my life.

Mid-night Sonnetesque

Now sleepily I lie, and wearily, drearily sigh.
With heavy eyelids, breaths, and limbs, I dream.
I'm floating down the Thames upon a stream
Of boats—but hark! Is that? A baby's cry.

Oh no! I sigh and moan and grip
The bedsheets up around my head—
I really want to stay in bed.
But, out I tumble—up!—and trip

Into pajamas waiting there
Beside the bed, upon the chair
Where in the dark no need to see
Have I, for it is certainty

That I'm on call each night to feed
My baby girl; I'm all she needs.

Sweetie

I've got a girl who's sweet as puddin'
I've got a girl who's sweet as pie
Pity any sweet-toothed boy in the city
'Cause Sweetie is the apple of her daddy's eye.

Boy Sonnet

I thought to write a sonnet for my sons
About the men they'll one day grow to be
And how I see in each of them the runs
Of greatness flowing from their fam'ly tree.

I thought to write about integrity,
And to encourage them in godly ways;
How sacrifice in love is just the key;
To be e'er slow to cut and quick to praise.

I thought to write of courage sure and strong:
To bravely lead in spite of dreadful fear,
To choose the right when all around choose wrong,
To take a stand for those whom God holds dear.

But if I'll reach their hearts and not their heads,
Then I must stoop to play Minecraft instead.

Kisser of Knees

I am the Kisser of Knees,
For my magic doth quickly appease
The wails and the cries
Of the two-foot-tall size
Who tend to get tripped up with ease.

A TCK Mom Dilemma

They have two names, dear little one,
These things and sounds and feelings.

Which shall I teach you, little one?

All that which from my native tongue
Holds for me depth of meaning?

Or that which, foreign though to me,
Communicates here easily?

It's Going to Be a Good Day
Inspired by Mitzi Pierce

Today's going to be a good day.

I may not have slept (again), but
Today's going to be a good day.

The kids may be fighting (again), but
Today's going to be a good day.

The house may be a mess (again), but
Today's going to be a good day.

We may be running late (again), but
Today's going to be a good day.

People may judge me (again), but
Today's going to be a good day.

I may be on my own (again), but
Today's going to be a good day.

And if it's not,
God's mercies will be new again tomorrow.

Diaper Haiku III

Sunday morning rush:
for once we're all on time, but
plans are soiled again.

Too Quiet?

Crash! Bang! Pow!
Rattle-Rattle
Pop!
Crack! Thud! Waaah!

These kids don't ever stop.

Bump, Squish
"Eeew!"
Stomp, Crush
Slam!
Clatter, Clatter
"Mom!"
Fling, Throw, Ram!

Bounce, Splat,
Thump!
Thunder, Rumble,
Flush!
Shatter, Crunch
Squeal!

My brain has turned to mush.

Crash! Bang!
Thud.

Silence strings along.

I should check this out.
It's too quiet—
Something's wrong.

In the Silence

The light seeps in
Through the cracks in the blinds
And into my consciousness.
The house is silent.

A chittering sound outside the window
Rouses me from rest,
Calling me to wakefulness.

I slip from the bed
And steal down the stairs,
Hoping to keep this silence to myself.

I open the blinds
And welcome in the light,
Orange glow upon the cushions
And the treetops.

I sit in the quiet,
Alone,
Yet never alone.

That insistent little bird
Outside the window
Is chirping reminders:

The One who loves me more
Is right here.

Unlucky

It's date night.
We both left our cell phones at home.

Unlucky?

We both look up and lock eyes.
Maybe not.

Whosoever Planteth a Tree

Whosoever
planteth a tree
p l a n t e t h in h o p e.
In a world of the instant,
the p l a n t i n g of a tree
is an act of sheer defiance —
a s t a t e m e n t to the world
that s i g n i f i c a n t things
take t i m e to g r o w:
r e l a t i o n s h i p s
m a t u r i t y
w i s d o m
children
wealth
faith
trust
skill
you
me

Summer Storm

To the garden I must go:
Days have passed since last I hoed.

Neighbor girls come watch the babes.
Sneaking out, I hide my face.

Strolling to our plot of land,
Bowl and knife and phone in hand,

See the clouds are piling higher:
Blues and grays and shades much whiter.

I can work in silence now,
Feel the sweat upon my brow.

Is that thunder? Have to hurry.
Further rumbles make me scurry.

Pick the squash, zucchini, too.
Check the melon stems. Achoo!

Drip then drop, I hear them plop,
Warning me to simply stop.

Eye the row of mounds to go:
I can do this. Maybe... No.

Yield myself to drenching fate:
Ripened produce cannot wait.

Pluck and gather, pile them high;
Hear the whoosh and rushing sigh.

Snatch the bowl and turn toward home,
Gem-drops falling on my nose.

Hear the rain fall faster now;
Run for trees and keep head down.

Cross the yard in flip-flop run.
Angry clouds obscure the sun.

Reach the back door just in time:
Skies wide open, downpour shines.

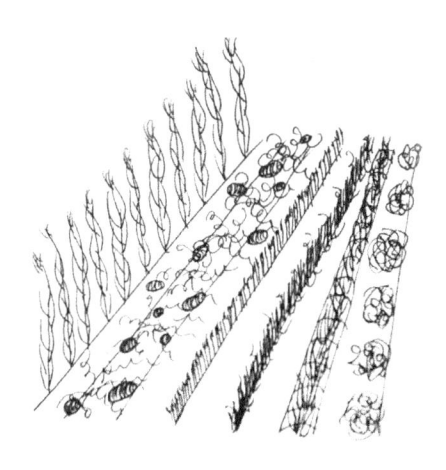

On the Paradox of Sleep

Sleep begets sleep.
I know this is true:
When I tuck you in early
You sleep the night through;
But if you're up late
Then early you rise
And sleepies hang heavy
In both of our eyes.

Diaper Haiku IV

Orange streak up-shot,
soiling dress and back and seat
again untimely.

It's Too Private

Did you know there's a poop chart?

> A what?

A poop chart. Assigned numbers based on texture and--ease of passage.

> Are you kidding me?

I know, right?

> Why have I never heard of this?!

Shhh—people don't talk about it.

> If I had a dollar for every conversation about poop we've had since the kids were born, I could retire now.

I know, I know.

> People should know about this.

Good luck bringing that up in conversation.

The Blue Car

        I don't know why
     it always has to be the

Blue   Car.
We have twenty-seven to choose from.
They could each have a baker's dozen, but
  they   each
  only   want
  that   one.

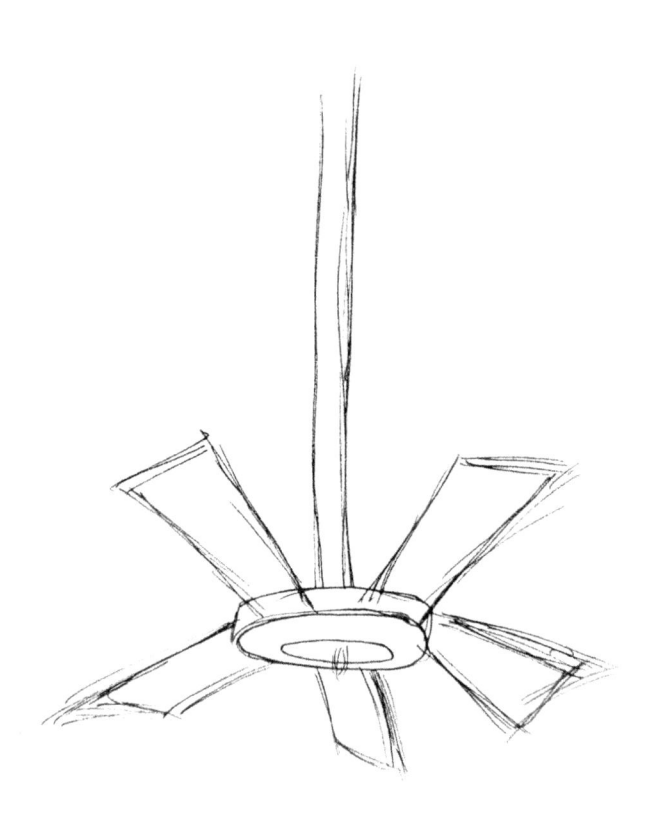

Another Morning

The five blades of the fan,
Splayed like jelly-covered fingers
Of the toddler who lives in the next room,
Spin above my head
As I muster the energy to get out of bed
And begin another day.

Father, give me strength for the messes.
And thank you for the reminder
To buy more jelly.
And thank you for jelly.
And toddlers.

Days of the Week

Monday, Tuesday,
Wednesday, Thursday,
Friday, Saturday, Sunday

Day after day
We name the days
Until he knows them all.

At first he would listen,
Then he'd repeat them,
Now he can say them along.

lunes, martes,
miércoles, jueves,
viernes, sábado, domingo

He's only four,
Let's teach him more.
His brain's a little sponge.

As long as he's
At home with me,
My teaching's never done.

Sustenance

Spirited solicitude
Swinish suckling
Small shape
Soft smells
Sustained swallows
Smooth strokes
Serene soothing
Submissive surrender
Safe snuggles
Sudden smile
Sleepy satiety
Satisfied sighs
Sweet slumber

The Law of Inevitability

Put these boys
together
in any room

and it's
just
a matter
of
T
I
M
E

before a fight breaks out.

I Wonder

I wonder as I wander—
why did I enter this room?

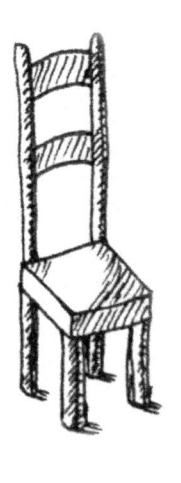

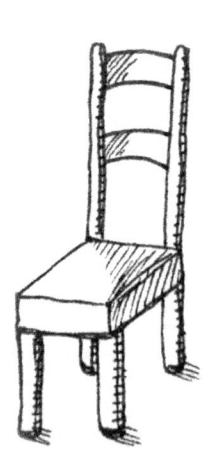

Shucking Corn

We sit together, shucking corn—
Together—
In high-backed wooden chairs around
The basket piles of shucks and strings.
We pass the cobs and bits of knowledge hand to hand.

The wrinkled ones work ably, nimbly,
Piling corn as fades the summer sun;
The small new hands are plump and clumsy,
Prone to halt their work in search of fun.

"Uh-oh, Grandma, this one has a worm."
"Let me show you what you have to do."
And so the wisdom passes ever onward,
From your great-grandparents down to you.

I'm taking mental notes so I'll remember
How to do this after they've passed on,
When I'm the wrinkled hands, and all the plump ones
Belong to your daughters and your sons.

Hide and Seek

My secret place: I scarcely breathe
Lest they find out my reprieve
Hiding 'hind the bathroom door.
Leave me be here? Nevermore.

A moment yet, the house is quiet
Though I know that soon they'll riot
Seeing I'm not at my chores,
Not folding clothes or cleaning floors.

Hark! Is that a voice I hear?
Ringing, singing loud and clear?
"I think Mom just went upstairs
To use the bathroom. Try the door."

One by one I hear them coming,
Searching, calling, and then drumming,
Drumming on the bathroom door.
Shall I answer? Nevermore.

Maybe if I sit in silence
Contemplating noncompliance
They will shortly give up and
Leave drumming on my bathroom door.

But instead they try the lock,
Then tap, tap, tap, and knock, knock, knock,
Rapping hard upon the surface
Of my little bathroom door.

Then I spy four little fingers
Reaching, stretching as I linger,
Trying hard to creep beneath
The shelter of my bathroom door.

There, in my exasperation,
I respond to their impatience:
"Leave me be!" I call to them
From there inside my bathroom door.

"But Mom, I'm hungry!" cries a voice,
Soon followed by a crashing noise
As fighting breaks out just outside
The safety of my bathroom door.

The children are there waiting still,
Determined not to leave until
I open up the bathroom door.
Will I have peace? No, nevermore.

Fun

The doors are all locked
The kids are tucked in
Now close all the drapes
Let the fun begin!

Bring out the Lucky Charms
Bring out the wine
Bring out the chocolate—
Tonight, we dine.

Put on a movie
Snuggle down deep
Forgive me if maybe I
Fall fast asl—

Diaper Haiku V

O Source of foul smells,
what dost thou teach me about
my humanity?

True Love

How do you love me? Let me count the ways.
You love me to the depth and breadth and height
Of the vomit buckets you change at night
And the child-free moments you give my days.
And in those seasons when I need much grace,
Or when I want to hide away and write,
You cover for me like a shining knight,
Or give me knowing looks and ample space.
Your tender touch has never once abused,
But strongly held my hand in search of faith,
Pursued my heart as if you'd always choose
To spend each day with me, and every breath,
Providing for my needs until we lose
The sweetness of our bond only through death.

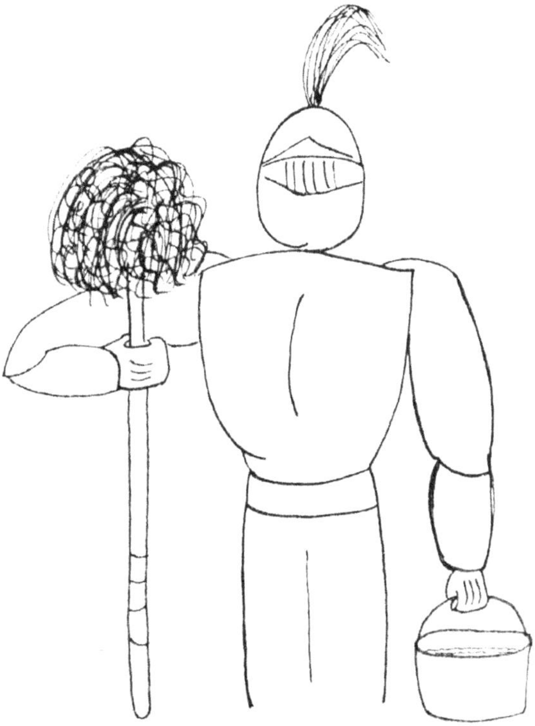

Failure

You can't do this, he said to me.
(Or was it I?)
You'll never be able to do this.

I tried to argue back,
But the words turned over and over in my mind.
It was an embarrassing failure for one such as I.

Just give up. What's the point?
The proposition was tempting.

You'll lose your family over this.
It seemed a logical end.

You're a failure.
I believed him.

Look at what you're costing your family.
They're better off without you.
You can't do this.
You're alone.

I tried to push through,
Carrying on with my day and my tasks,
But I ended up in the middle of the bed,
Sitting and sobbing and wishing for a way out.

I tried to hear another Voice, but I couldn't.
The thoughts swirled louder and louder,
My own voice mixing with the other,
Until I could not discern betwixt the two.

I cried myself to sleep.

His mercies are new every morning.

I awoke with new resolve,
Turning once again to the small book on my side table.
I soaked up the words while all was quiet
In my head and in my home.

I ate and I drank and I prepared myself.
Not many days later, it was time to try again.

Failure, he said to me.
You can't do this.
You're alone.

He was right, to some degree.
I failed the test again.
But this time I was listening for Another's Voice.

I love you, He said to me.
I have already succeeded for you.
Listen for what I have to teach you in this.
You are not alone—I will never leave you.

I believed Him.
I sat in the middle of the bed again,
Same place, same circumstances,
But this time clothed in peace and a right mind.

When test time came again, I was ill.
Feverish, sick, unrested and weak,
I was incapable of success on my own.

You'll fail again, he said.
No, *I can do all things through Christ who strengthens me.*

You're alone, he said.
No, *He promised, I will never leave you or forsake you.*

I had to stand and wait,
My sickly body subjected to the elements.

Upon my turn I asked silently for help,
I got behind the wheel,
And I drove.

Like pouring water over a dry altar,
Filling the trenches to remove all doubt,
My fever, the delay—
All worked to prove the impossibility
And His perfect Ability.

By His grace,
In the power of His Spirit,
I succeeded.

Give me your failures, He says.
I will redeem them.

Wiping

Runny noses
Sticky hands
Crumby highchairs
Messy floors
Crusty counters
Scribbly walls
Smudgy windows
Streaky mirrors
Splatty toilets
Dirty bottoms
Stinky armpits
Muddy feet

Muddy feet

Misty eyes

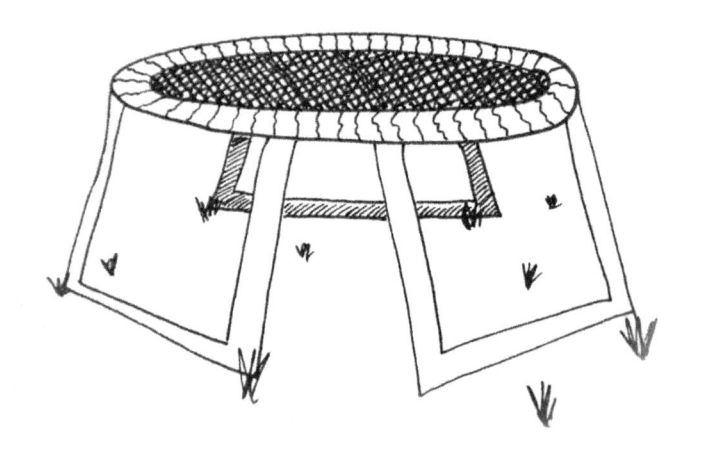

Trampoline

I climbed onto the trampoline
Because jumping looked more fun
Than standing in the sun
And waiting.

"This is the best day ever!" he said.

Better than swimming
        In the Mediterranean Sea
Or cheering the parade
        Of trucks with candy.

Better than playing
        At Chuck E. Cheese
Or coming face-to-face
        With the king of beasts.

It was just a simple thing:
Jumping on a trampoline
With Mom.

At the Beach

All I really want to do
Is just relax, enjoy the view
With a book in my hand and my feet in the sand
At the beach.

        Put our things on the mat,
        Spray sunscreen, don a hat,
        Kick off shoes, spray some more:
        Sunscreen child two, three, four.

I glance at my book,
But I hear, "Mommy, look!"
And the child who is three
Is soon swallowed by sea.

        In helping, I'm wet,
        So my book I forget,
        And I stay in the sea
        While they splash-play with glee.

Once thoroughly chilled,
I sit down while they build
Castle moats in the sand.
Reach for book with my hand...

        But then, "I'm hungry, Mom!"
        Slices through the brief calm
        And my hand finds the food
        That I packed for our brood.

Once all mouths are well fed
And the food put to bed,
"Mommy, I need to go!"
Says an urgent voice, low.

          So we two tramp and rove
          To the loo and he goes,
          Then we slog through the sand
          To our mat, hand in hand.

"Mommy, let's take a hike!"
Says another young tike
When he sees me return.
"But you promised!" he burns.

          Down the coast we both roam,
          Over rocks, through the foam,
          Till it's time to turn back
          And help Daddy to pack.

Rinse our feet, shake out hair,
There is sand EVERYWHERE,
Stuff our towels and the bread
With the book that's unread.

          Hold my hand, home we go.
          Why's your face all aglow?
          "Mom, today was the best!
          What a great way to rest!"

What I Meant to Say

When I said
"Good morning, Sunshine!"

And when I said
"There's my girl."

And when I said
"You make my day."

What I meant to say is
"I love you."

Disaster

One day I felt
Particularly brave,
So I tackled Stuff-Mart
With all four kids in tow
For the first—and last—time.

I timed it perfectly between naps,
Fed them snacks on the way,
Gave them jobs to do,
Promised treats at home,
And prayed.

The kids were well-behaved,
Surprising even me,
But still
We had an overturned stroller
(With the newborn strapped inside)
And a bleeding head wound
From a spinning kindergartener
Who collided with a cart
As I reached for the last item
On our short list.

Any time I get that feeling again,
Of being particularly brave,
I shake my head.
"Don't do it,"
I tell myself.
"It's going to end in disaster."

One day,
Maybe I'll listen.

Lost

Lost:

One sane and rational mind

Capable of multi-tasking
Discussing lofty ideas
Calculating basic math
And remembering details.

Last seen in 2007
At the corner of Marriage and Motherhood.

If found, please contact
The woman who entered this room and forgot why.

Going Somewhere

The kids are home from school,
Age ten and six (and four and one).
The boys have argued all day long
    Until I've had enough.
            "We're going to take a walk,
            So grab your shoes and coat," I chide.
            A fight breaks out again until
            I send them on outside.

    I close the door, but then
    I step back in to get my keys;
    The fight continues in the yard
        Among the neighbor's leaves.
            I yell and fuss at them
            For their unkind and hateful ways,
            Lamenting how I have to tend
            To children every day.

    We start our silent walk,
    But soon begin discussing how
    The yellowjackets' nest nearby
        Is buried underground.
            "Look at those trees!" I say,
            "Consider well their shape and hue,
            For when we come back home again
            We'll paint a tree or two."

We walk through woods and down
The driveway by the oak and shed,
And soon our steps are headed back
    Among the Fall seedbeds.
            I look down at the boys,
            Who now are walking next to me
            And marvel at the simple change
            Brought on by scenery.

    Their hands are tucked in mine,
Their fighting ceased in wonderment,
    And softly, swiftly we turn home,
        Excited and content.

Little One Lost
For Kate, and Gideon Joseph Speer

Little One,
I do not know you,
Neither form nor feature.

I do not know you,
But I love you.

I know you not;
Know only the hopes and dreams
I had for you.

I carried your life
Within mine
For a time,

And I carry still
The name that I gave to you
As a token of hope:

One day
I will meet you,
And you will know your mother.

First Day in Ramah
By D.A. Speer

What is a choice between horror and sorrow?
In the stillness of morning we mourn on the morrow.
How could it be that we'd not know your face?
Left shaking in violent wrath at the grave.

After all this, after all, after all,
A voice heard in Ramah,
A mother's dread call.
Can word seek to comfort,
Could any balm sway
The anger, exhaustion, and rage at the grave?

Not alone, never doubted;
Not alone, but dejected.

The stone, alive, that the builders rejected
Will not break the bruised and afflicted.

Approaching, weeping, full of fury,
Storming within and without at the enemy,
Innocence lost in the echo of space—
Meets limitless power,
Unrestrained grace.

"If you'd have been here,
He would not have died."

"Death's not the end, my friend," He replied.

Flower of Mine

Dear little flower,
even as I lament
to cut you away
from the roots and leaves
which nourish your fleeting life,
I delight
in the arrangement
of your beauty
to grace this space
for one bright hour
in the bouquet
I am making.

What This Mother Needs

My children are not typical
(Emotional or physical)
And do not always do and say
The things you think they should;

But they are all incredible,
Delightful, complex, knowable,
All imaging the Maker just as
He designed they should.

Because they live outside the box
My children walk quite different walks,
So please forgive if I don't do
The things you think I should.

God has made me mom of these
Whose raising is without the ease
Of those whose minds are typical
And act just as they "should"

So give me courage, give me grace,
Help my heart to keep its place
Looking to Jehovah for
The daily Bread of motherhood;

For building one another up
Can overflow a brimming cup
And help the various Body parts
To function as they should

And that, my friend, is good.

Back in the Day

"Back in the day"
Is a way of saying
That what came before
Is somehow much better
Or much worse
Than what is now.

It's a way of comparing
The present
With the past
To make a point,

Like you should be thankful,
Or it's a shame,
Or I don't understand this generation.

I remember my grandparents saying it.
I've heard my parents utter it.
I now carry the refrain.

And one day
My children will repeat it
To their children's children

For there is nothing new under the sun.

Diaper Haiku VI

My bonnie lass made
yellow curds and yellow whey
of her mommy's milk.

Smiles I

The whole world smiles at Evelyn.
Indeed, how could it not?
Just look at that face,
She's a creature of grace;
A lovely, bright little spot.

The whole world smiles at Evelyn.
"She's beautiful!" they say.
Between you and me,
I tend to agree.
'Twas God who did make her that way.

The whole world smiles at Evelyn,
For everywhere we go
Both strangers and friends
Delight to no end
To see how she wrinkles her nose.

The whole world smiles at Evelyn,
And now she has the knack
Of coying her eyes
To look for surprise:
She's ready to smile right back.

Off Day

The children are off school again today,
Which means I'm on.

Diaper Haiku VII

That is not chocolate
My dear husband said to me
When I picked it up.

Found

Found:

One three-ring binder
Labeled "external brain"

Contains a detailed calendar,
School schedule,
Meal ideas,
Shopping lists,
Vaccine records,
Coloring pages,
A few elementary drawings,
And pink sticky note reminders:
    "Take a shower"
    "Make dental appointments"
    "Patch jeans"
    "Hide leftover candy!!"

If this belongs to you,
And you remember how to use a phone,
Call 9-1-1
And tell them you need assistance.

Laundry Day

Sort and wash
Dry and fold
Wash and dry and sort and fold
Fluff and hang
Fluff and fold
Wash and dry and sort and fold
Sort and—Hey!
WHO PUT POOP IN THE LAUNDRY BASKET?!?!?!?!?!

It's Only a Season

When they tell me
"It's only a season,"
I want to say,
"So is winter—
In North Dakota."

I Wanted to Write a Poem

I wanted to write a poem for you.
Something to delight your ears,
Or make you laugh,
Or cry,
Or think,
But the laundry is piled high,
And so is the kitchen sink,
And four little mouths are hungry again,
And I'm tired,
So tired,
So today,
This is all I have to offer.
It will have to be enough.
Please forgive my lack,
And maybe I'll have something more to give
Tomorrow.

Smiles II

I think of all the ones for whom
The world has never smiled:
The soul of dour countenance,
The problematic child,

The few whose scars are visible,
The many whose are not,
The lives abused, oppressed, misused:
The ones the world forgot,

Who've never grown in favor,
Or known a wealth of love,
Nor sensed they had security
At home or up above.

I think about the ones for whom
The world has never smiled,
And how our God created them
Just like my lovely child.

I wonder—could I give to them
A few smiles of my own
And grant them freely, patiently
The grace that I have known?

For had I never known the smiles
Of God through kith and kin,
I know there'd be no difference—
Deep down I'm just like them.

And maybe, had they known the smile
Of favor undeserved,
They'd all be different people now,
And less inclined to hurt.

So I will give out smiles and grace
And favor as I can,
Remembering what Christ gave me
When He became a man.

How I Will Be Remembered

If I am to be remembered
After I am gone,
It will be for the impact
Of my words,
And my actions,
Upon the life of another.

Positively,
Negatively,
Powerfully,
Personal.

If I am to influence
How I will be remembered
After I am gone,
I must measure the impact
Of my words
And my actions
Upon the life of another
Before I proceed.

Transformation

I stare at the brown-eyed girl in the picture
And wonder at who she's become.
Back then she was innocent, prideful, unbroken;
Today, those four kids call her Mom.
If only someone had pulled her aside
And warned her of what was to come.
But then, do you think she would really have listened?
I doubt it. How stubborn that one.
Some things are best learned through experience, I guess:
The grueling job of a mom.
This seasoning process has greatly transformed
The woman that I've now become.

On Waiting In Line

I stand in a line
That reaches far beyond my vision
To the beginning of things.
I know my place in it,
Coming after those who go before,
Preceding those who come behind.
We—all of us—
Shuffle forward
Step by faltering step,
Into the spot once occupied by another.
We—none of us—
Feel confident
In our occupation
Of the spot in which we stand.

It can be a difficult thing
To wait in line
And watch the passage
Of time
From time
To time,
Stepping ever nearer
To the end we cannot see.

We step,
With patience,
And step,
And experience,
And step,
And hope,
And step—

Suggested Reading

You may have noticed that some of my poems are playful parodies of well-known poems. Others might have a ring of something familiar, though you can't quite put your finger on it. No writer writes in a vacuum (although I have been known to poem while vacuuming). Let me introduce you to some of the many voices to whom I am indebted. If you enjoyed my poems, I expect you'll enjoy these even more:

Matsuo Basho
"Frog Haiku"

Elizabeth Barrett Browning
"How Do I Love Thee?" from *Sonnets for the Portuguese*

King David
Psalm 63

Emily Dickinson
"Chartless" and "A Bird Came Down the Walk"

T.S. Eliot
"Journey of the Magi" and "The Hollow Men"

Robert Frost
"The Road Not Taken"

Gerard Manley Hopkins
"Pied Beauty," "Carrion Comfort," and "God's Grandeur"

A.E. Housman
"Loveliest of Trees" from *A Shropshire Lad*

Lanier Ivester
"I Came By a Lane" in *The Molehill, Vol. 1*

A.A. Milne
"The Invaders," "Sand-Between-the-Toes," "Daffodowndilly," and others from *When We Were Very Young*

Edgar Allan Poe
"The Raven"

William Shakespeare
Sonnets 29 and 116 and 130

Percy Bysshe Shelley
"Ozymandias"

Robert Louis Stevenson
"Bed in Summer," "The Cow," "The Swing," and "To My Name-child" from *A Child's Garden of Verses*

Alfred, Lord Tennyson
"The Lady of Shalott"

William Carlos Williams
"The Red Wheelbarrow" from *Spring and All*

William Wordsworth
"I Wandered Lonely as a Cloud"

COME PLAY!

Are you a mom who likes to play with words, too?

Or if writing isn't your thing, maybe you like to paint,
Or sew,
Or throw pottery.

Or maybe you enjoy crafting food,
Or designing really awesome spreadsheets,
Or building elaborate forts and LEGO ships with the kids.

If you're in the trenches of motherhood,
come show us your creative outlet—

That thing that eases stress and delights your soul;
That one thing you're itching to create during nap time
(assuming sleep is not a pressing need).

[If you don't have a creative outlet, begin by coloring the title page!]

Then look me up on Instagram or Facebook --> **@rachelsdonahue**

And use this hashtag to show us how you play:
#CREATIVEMOMPLAY

Let's encourage one another and create something beautiful
in the land of Motherhood!